START EXPLORING

Trees

FACTS • ACTIVITIES • FUN

Godfrey Hall

Illustrated by Gordon Munro

CONTENTS

What is a tree?	2	Tree life	14
Looking for leaves	4	Working trees	16
Seeds and fruits	6	Treehouses	18
Changing seasons	8	Recycling	20
Fantastic trees	10	Saving the forests	22
Tree spotting	12	Glossary	24

Headway • Hodder & Stoughton

What is a tree?

Look out of the window. Can you see any trees? Trees can be found in towns, in parks, in the country and in gardens. They are large woody plants. A tree has lots of different parts.

twigs

branches

leaves

The stem of the tree is called the **trunk**. At the top of the trunk you will find the **branches**. Small branches are called **twigs**. At the end of the branches or twigs are the **leaves**.

trunk

The **roots** of a tree spread out under the ground. The roots help keep it alive.

roots

Now You See

See if you can grow a shelled peanut by planting one in some damp soil.

Put the nut in a flowerpot and cover it with some soil. Put a plastic bag over the pot and put it somewhere dark and warm for 14 to 21 days. Once it starts to produce a shoot, bring it out into the light.

Put it on a windowsill in the warm sunlight. Make sure you keep the soil damp. It will soon grow into a strong plant if you look after it.

Here is a tree trunk which has been sawn in two.

If you count the rings you can tell how old the tree is. How many rings can you see in this tree trunk?

AMAZING FACTS!

Acid rain is killing a large number of trees. In Germany in 1983, one in three trees was damaged by acid rain.

Looking for leaves

A good way of finding out the name of a tree is to look at the leaves. Here are some of the leaves you might find in the park or in your garden.

This is a holly leaf. It is tough and shiny. The edges are prickly. The leaf stays on the tree all through the year.

This is a leaf from a fir tree. Fir trees often grow in parks.

This is an oak leaf. Insects and small creatures like living under fallen oak leaves. The edges of the leaves are curved.

AMAZING FACTS!

The leaves of the bay tree have a strong smell if they are crumbled between your fingers. They are used in cooking.

This special-shaped leaf comes from the horse chestnut. This tree is found in parks and streets.

This leaf comes from the lime tree. It has jagged edges. It is called a **simple leaf**. Lime trees can be found in parks and cities. During the summer lots of tiny insects live on the leaves. This makes the leaves sticky with **honeydew**.

The leaves of a willow tree are long and thin. They have short stalks. Willow trees usually grow where it is wet or damp.

Now You See

Put a leaf between two pieces of newspaper and put something heavy on top of it. Leave it for two days. Take out your pressed leaf and stick it onto a card using some sticky tape.

Seeds and fruits

The **seed** is the part of a tree from which a new tree will grow. The **fruit** is the part of a tree that holds the seed.

Here are some of the fruits from trees you might find in your garden or in the park.

Look carefully at them.

◀ This is the fruit of the horse chestnut. The seed is called a **conker**. You can see it inside the case. Cows like to eat conkers.

AMAZING FACTS!

The silver birch has fruit called **catkins**. These hang down from the branches of the tree and feel furry.

▲ This is the winged fruit of the sycamore tree. It turns as it falls to the ground like a helicopter's rotor blades.

▲ This is an **acorn**. It is the fruit of the oak tree. Squirrels like collecting acorns to store during the winter.

Now You See

Make your own 'heli seed'

1. Cut out a piece of paper 10 x 3 cms. Fold it lengthways along the middle.

2. Open it out and make a cut 3 cms long down the fold from one of the short sides of the paper.

3. Make another cut half way along the long edge of one side of the paper into the fold in the centre. Fold it underneath itself.

4. Fix the narrow end with a paperclip. Fold the two tabs at the other end in opposite directions so that they are at right angles to the paper clip end. Then let your 'heli seed' fall!

Changing seasons

Some trees lose their leaves in winter, but others keep their leaves all the year round.

Trees that lose their leaves are called **deciduous**. The leaves drop off in the autumn. The tree stops making food and rests for the winter.

This is an oak in winter.

Trees that keep their leaves are called **evergreen**. The leaves are often tough and shiny so that they can stand the cold weather. Others are thin like needles.

Here are some trees that lose their leaves for the winter.

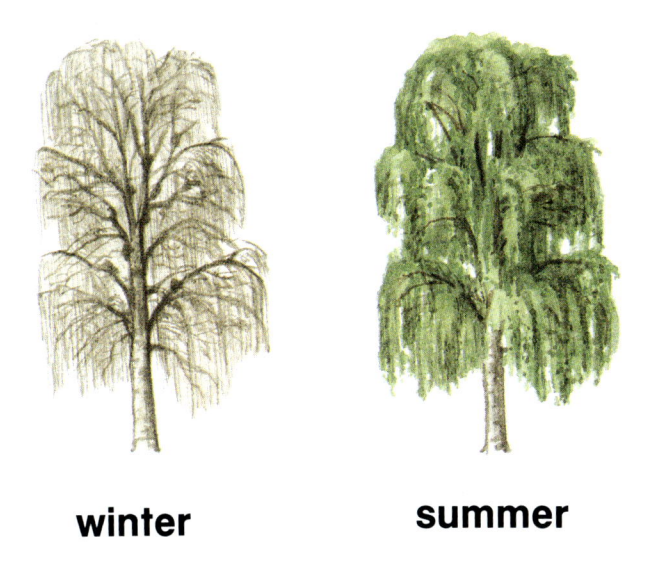

The ash has strong wood. It grows in hedgerows and woods.

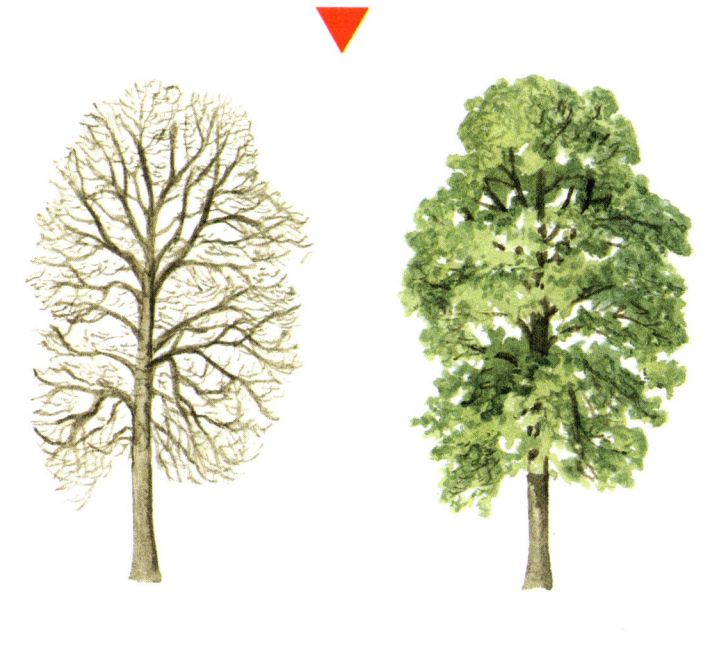

winter　　　summer

The silver birch has a silvery bark which peels off. It grows in parks and gardens.

winter　　　summer

A lombardy poplar in winter.

A lombardy poplar in summer.

This is a poplar tree. You can grow a tiny poplar tree from a twig. Put it in water, and when it has grown some roots, put it in some soil.

AMAZING FACTS!

Orange trees are evergreens and have large, glossy leaves.

Fantastic trees

There are some very strange trees growing in different parts of the world.

Redwoods are the largest trees in the world. They can grow over 100 metres tall. These giant trees grow in California in the USA where they are called Sequoias. They are the largest living things on the earth.

The gum tree or eucalyptus tree of Australia is unusual because after it blossoms the flowers turn into 'gum nuts'. There are over 500 types of gum trees. Koalas love the leaves of the blue gum trees. Some red gum trees are thought to be over one thousand years old.

After a bush fire the blackbutt gum tree will produce lots of new young plants.

The banyan tree grows in warm parts of the world such as India and Pakistan. The branches are held up by special roots. These are called **prop roots**. They grow down to the ground.

Palm trees flower and bear fruit at the same time. We get coconuts from palm trees. They grow in hot countries.

AMAZING FACTS!

The cannonball tree of South America has fruit that look just like cannonballs!

Tree spotting

If you are going tree spotting you will need a notebook and a pencil.

Look at the shape of the tree and its leaf.

Does the tree have any flowers or fruit on it?

What kind of bark does the tree have? Is it rough or is it smooth?

Broad-leaved trees often look like this.

Keep a record like this:

fruit

bark

oak tree

leaf

Now You See

Find a tree. Take a piece of paper. Fix it to the tree with some tape. Use the side of a wax crayon and rub it on the paper from the top to bottom.

Make a tree habitat

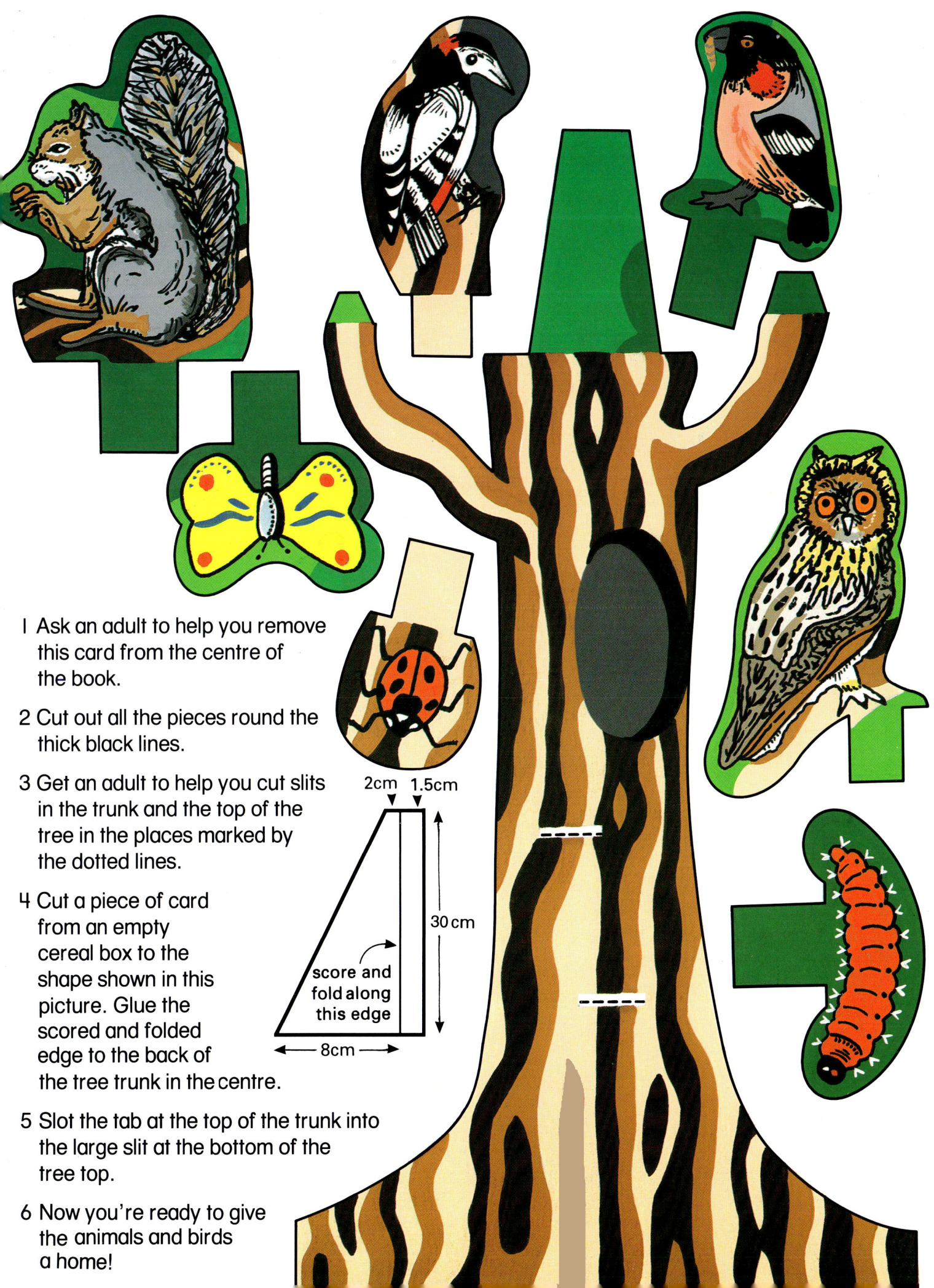

1. Ask an adult to help you remove this card from the centre of the book.

2. Cut out all the pieces round the thick black lines.

3. Get an adult to help you cut slits in the trunk and the top of the tree in the places marked by the dotted lines.

4. Cut a piece of card from an empty cereal box to the shape shown in this picture. Glue the scored and folded edge to the back of the tree trunk in the centre.

5. Slot the tab at the top of the trunk into the large slit at the bottom of the tree top.

6. Now you're ready to give the animals and birds a home!

2cm 1.5cm

30 cm

score and fold along this edge

← 8cm →

Conifers or fir trees look like this.

AMAZING FACTS!

The monkey puzzle tree has a very strange bark and sharp leaves.

Go round your garden or the park and see if you can spot any oak, fir, willow or horse chestnut trees. Colour in a box for each tree you find.

	Oak	Fir	Willow	Horse Chestnut
5				
4				
3				
2				
1				

Tree life

Birds build nests in the branches of the tree and small animals make their homes in holes and around the roots.

A tree is like a small town or village. It has lots of small creatures that live around the bottom in the dead leaves and under pieces of wood.

There are also other creatures that live on or under the bark of the tree.

Slugs like the damp wet places under trees. They have long tongues that they use to chew with. There are hundreds of teeth on their tongues.

Pill woodlouse

You will often find **woodlice** under a tree in the dead leaves or under a piece of rotten wood. The pill woodlouse rolls up when it is frightened.

Black slug

14

Caterpillars are often very brightly coloured so that birds and other creatures will not eat them. Caterpillars are the larval stage of a butterfly or moth.

The caterpillar of the tiger moth is very hairy and when the caterpillar is touched it rolls up into a ball to protect itself. It is sometimes called a 'woolly bear'.

Tiger moth caterpillar

A group of sawfly caterpillars can eat a whole bush if given the chance.

If you collect some of these tiny creatures to look at, wear gloves and make sure that you put them back where you found them. Remember it is their home!

AMAZING FACTS!

The floor of the rain forest is full of many strange creatures such as the bird-eating spider.

Treehouses

Look up at a tree, and you'll probably be able to spot an animal's home in it. Squirrels build their homes in trees. They are called **dreys**. They are often very untidy. There are two types of squirrel in Britain - the Grey and the Red. If they ever meet they fight. Red squirrels are found where there are lots of pine trees.

AMAZING FACTS!

Raccoons from the USA like making their homes in holes in trees. They often spend the winter in these holes.

Woodpeckers make their homes in the trunks of trees. They use their strong beaks to make holes in the bark.

Caterpillars are often very brightly coloured so that birds and other creatures will not eat them. Caterpillars are the larval stage of a butterfly or moth.

The caterpillar of the tiger moth is very hairy and when the caterpillar is touched it rolls up into a ball to protect itself. It is sometimes called a 'woolly bear'.

Tiger moth caterpillar

A group of sawfly caterpillars can eat a whole bush if given the chance.

If you collect some of these tiny creatures to look at, wear gloves and make sure that you put them back where you found them. Remember it is their home!

AMAZING FACTS!

The floor of the rain forest is full of many strange creatures such as the bird-eating spider.

Working trees

Lots of the fruit we eat comes from trees. In Kent in south-east England, there are orchards full of apple trees. In cooler countries, pear and plum trees are grown. In hot countries, orange, lemon and grapefruit trees are grown. Trees can also give us other things such as cork and rubber.

Apple tree

Some apples are sweet to eat, some are sour. The apple tree belongs to the same family as the rose. Apples are picked in the autumn. In spring, apple trees are covered with pink and white blossom.

Lemon tree

Lemon trees grow in warm parts of the world. They have sweet-smelling white flowers. The fruit have tough yellow skins and are full of juice which is very good for you.

Now You See

1 Go into your local shop or supermarket and see if you can spot any fruits that come from trees.

Cork tree

Cork is used to make tiles and stoppers for bottles. It is usually taken from the bark of the cork oak which is found in Spain and North Africa. The outside of the bark is used.

Rubber tree

Rubber comes from a thick liquid inside the tree. This liquid is collected by making a cut in the bark of the tree and putting a cup below to catch the liquid as it drips out. Rubber trees grow in tropical countries.

2 Put a cork from a bottle in a bowl of water. Does it float?

AMAZING FACTS!

The prunes you buy in the shops are actually dried plums!

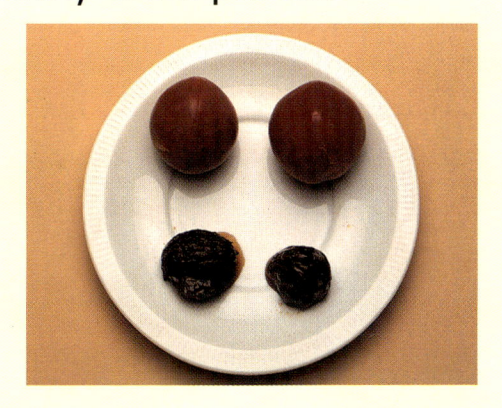

Treehouses

Look up at a tree, and you'll probably be able to spot an animal's home in it. Squirrels build their homes in trees. They are called **dreys**. They are often very untidy. There are two types of squirrel in Britain - the Grey and the Red. If they ever meet they fight. Red squirrels are found where there are lots of pine trees.

AMAZING FACTS!

Raccoons from the USA like making their homes in holes in trees. They often spend the winter in these holes.

Woodpeckers make their homes in the trunks of trees. They use their strong beaks to make holes in the bark.

Rooks make their homes high in the trees. They nest together in **rookeries** as they like living together. The nests can be very untidy. They build them high up so that they are safe.

There are even some people who make their own treehouses. These are often built in the fork of a tree and have a special ladder to get to them from the ground.

Now You See

Collect together some cardboard boxes and containers. Use these to make your own model treehouse. See if you can make a ladder for it and some furniture.

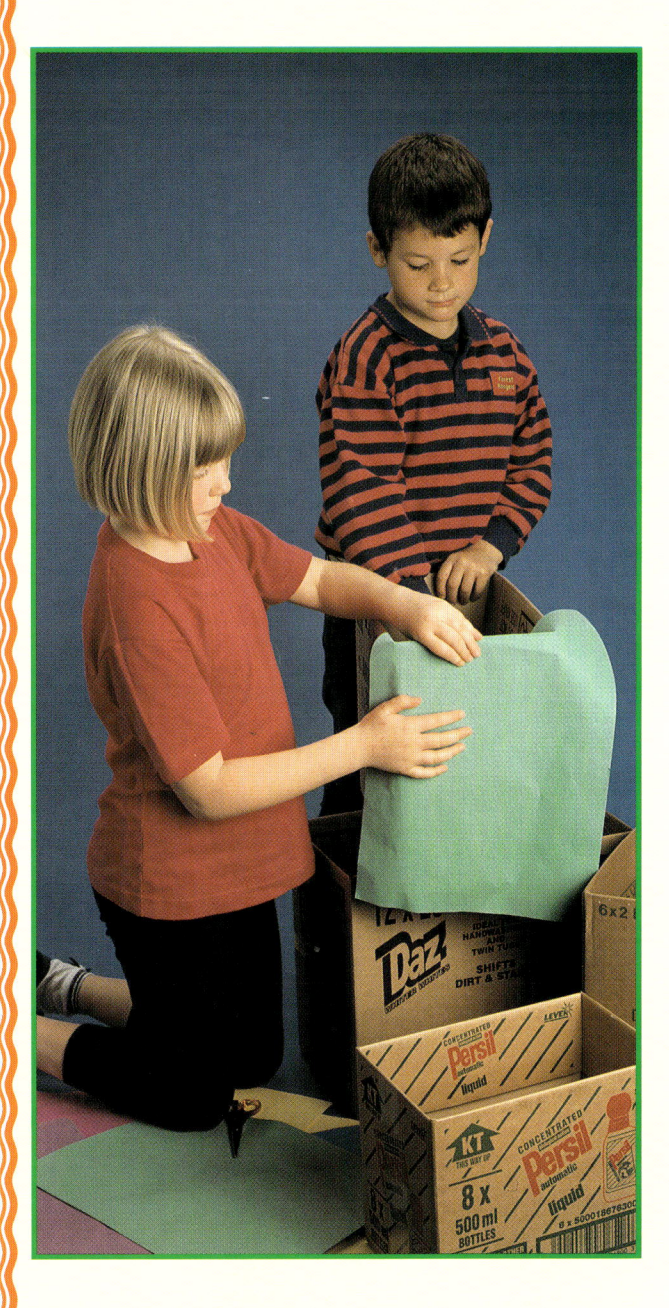

Recycling

Wood from trees is made into many different things. One of the most important of these is paper.

To make paper, logs must first have the bark taken off. They are then chopped into tiny pieces. These pieces are mixed with chemicals to make a wood pulp. A lot of wood has to be used to make paper.

It is possible to recycle paper that has been used already to make new paper.

If we recycle 1 tonne of waste paper we will help save over 15 trees.

The best wood for making paper comes from pine or spruce trees.

There are lots of pine forests in Sweden and Finland. ▼

AMAZING FACTS!

By the end of the twentieth century, one in three of all the trees in the tropical rain forests will have been destroyed.

Now You See

Mix some flour and water in a small pot until it is quite thick. Cut up an old newspaper into tiny pieces. Mix the flour paste into a bucket of water and stir it up. Add the newspaper and mix it together. This is papier mâché. Leave it for a few hours. Squeeze out the water from your pulp and squeeze it into a shape. Put the shape somewhere warm to dry. Leave it for 3 or 4 days, and then see what has happened to it.

We use a lot of paper. We have to save trees so we must be careful not to waste paper and put our old newspapers and comics into the special paper skips. Have you got one at your school?

Saving the forests

Trees are important because they use up a gas in the air called **carbon dioxide** and give out **oxygen** which we need to breathe.

Large parts of tropical forests are being burnt and used for roads, making fields and breeding cattle.

If people go on cutting down the forests then the air will begin to change. Scientists are worried that this will change the weather and make the earth hotter.

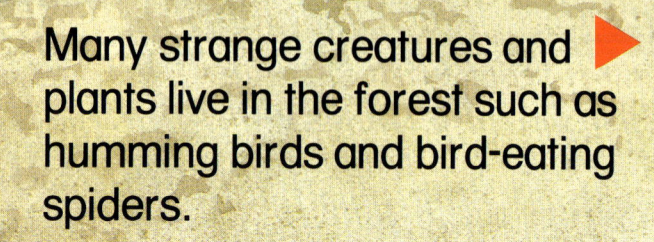

Many strange creatures and plants live in the forest such as humming birds and bird-eating spiders.

22

Now You See

Plant an orange or lemon pip in a pot of compost. Make sure the soil is damp. Cover it with a plastic bag and put it somewhere warm. Wait for the first shoots to appear.

The trees in a tropical rainforest are very tall and have big roots.

They flower and fruit at the same time. Often the flowers grow straight out of the tree trunk.

AMAZING FACTS!

Every 5 minutes, an area of forest the size of 1,000 football pitches is destroyed somewhere in the world.

GLOSSARY

blossom These are the flowers on a tree. They produce the seeds. Most trees need insects to carry pollen from one flower to the next. This pollen helps the flowers make the seeds.

chemicals These are used to help make some types of wood pulp. Wood pieces are put with chemicals in huge tanks to cook.

compost This is a mixture of soil and other things. It is used to grow seeds and plants. You may have a compost heap in your garden. This will be full of rich soil.

grapefruit A large yellow fruit with a fleshy inside, a bit like an orange but bigger. People often eat grapefruit for their breakfast. It has a lot of goodness inside it.

hedgerow A row of hedges. Hedgerows are often full of life with birds nesting, and small creatures making their homes under the hedge. Insects like hedgerows as there can be damp, dark spots underneath.

humming bird This is a small tropical bird that makes its wings move very quickly making a humming sound.

liquid This is something that moves, like water and oil. It flows along, and has no proper shape. Lemonade and milk are both liquids.

skip This is a large container used for holding rubbish or other things. You will often see skips being carried on the back of lorries.

spider This is an eight-legged creature that traps its prey in a web. It spins the web using tiny silk threads.

tropical If something comes from a tropical part of the world, then it will be from somewhere very hot. Tropical forests are often hot and wet all the year round.

wood pulp This is used to make paper. Wood pulp is made by chopping up the logs after the bark has been taken off. This is done by a special chopping machine.